Related by adoption

A handbook for grandparents and other relatives

Hedi Argent

BAAF
ADOPTION
& FOSTERING

Published by
British Association for Adoption & Fostering
(BAAF)
Saffron House
6–10 Kirby Street
London EC1N 8TS
www.baaf.org.uk

Charity registration 275689 (England and Wales)
and SCO39337 (Scotland)

British Library Cataloguing in Publication Data
A catalogue record for this book is available from
the British Library

ISBN 978 1 910039 03 8

Project management by Jo Francis, BAAF
Photographs on cover and in book posed by
models (except on p.57).
Designed by Andrew Haig & Associates
Typeset by Fravashi Aga
Printed in Great Britain by T J International
Trade distribution by Turnaround Publisher
Services, Unit 3, Olympia Trading Estate,
Coburg Road, London N22 6TZ

BAAF is the leading UK-wide membership
organisation for all those concerned with
adoption, fostering and child care issues.

Contents

Acknowledgements

I am grateful to the late Daphne Batty, Jeffrey Coleman, and Phillida Sawbridge for their helpful comments on successive drafts of this handbook. I also want to thank Shaila Shah, Director of Publications at BAAF, and Jo Francis, for their unfailing patience and support. Finally, I am most indebted to all the adopters, grandparents and other relatives who have so generously shared their stories and whose voices can be heard throughout this book.

Hedi Argent
January 2004

This edition

This third edition of *Related by Adoption* has been comprehensively revised and updated in line with recent legislative changes.

Notes about the authors

Hedi Argent is an independent family placement consultant, trainer and freelance writer. She is the author of *Find me a Family* (Souvenir Press, 1984), *Whatever Happened to Adam?* (BAAF, 1998), *Related by Adoption* (BAAF, 2004), *One of the Family* (BAAF, 2005), *Ten Top Tips for Placing Children in Permanent Families* (BAAF, 2006), J*osh and Jaz have Three Mums* (BAAF, 2007), *Ten Top Tips for Placing Siblings* (BAAF, 2008), and T*en Top Tips for Supporting Kinship Placements* (BAAF, 2009). She is the co-author of *Taking Extra Care* (BAAF, 1997, with Ailee Kerrane) and *Dealing with Disruption* (BAAF, 2006, with Jeffrey Coleman), and the editor of *Keeping the Doors Open* (BAAF, 1988), *See You Soon* (BAAF, 1995), *Staying Connected* (BAAF, 2002), and *Models of Adoption Support* (BAAF, 2003). She has also written six illustrated booklets in the children's series published by BAAF: *What Happens in Court?* (2003, with Mary Lane), *What is Contact?* (2004), *What is a Disability?* (2004), *Life Story Work* (2005, with Shaila Shah), *What is Kinship Care?* (2007), *Adopting a Brother or Sister* (2010), and *Where are my Brothers and Sisters?* (2010).

Introduction

I do think children need a family and that's more than just a mum or a mum and dad. Jean's adopted children have got me and Auntie Mary and a granddad and their uncle and his wife – that's another auntie – and a cousin who lives further away with her family.
Grandparent of adopted children

Adoption is a good way of building a family but it is different from having children born into the family. For grandparents there can be no poignant rush of familiarity – the child will not have your daughter's eyes or your son's habit of wrinkling his nose. Some of the joy of grandparenthood lies in the evident continuity of the generations. Some of the satisfaction of belonging to an extended family lies in the recognition that aunts and uncles and cousins have similarities that demonstrate the enduring nature of the family. But the adopted child comes from another line and adoption is proof that not all families endure.

One out of every three of us is, or will be, a grandparent. Approximately one out of every 75 people in the UK is adopted. This means that a very large number of people are grandparents or otherwise related to children who have been adopted.

Adoption today

At the beginning of the 21st century we see and hear a great deal about adoption in the newspapers and on television. Adoption is encouraged by government and pursued by all local authorities and voluntary agencies as the most permanent solution for children in the care system who cannot return to live with their birth families. Adoption by step-parents and adoption of children from overseas adds to the number of adopted young people in Britain today.

Sixty years ago it was thought that adoption was a one-off event, a new start for all concerned and children, most of them small babies, could be brought up without knowing that they were adopted. Generally grandparents and other relatives kept the secret and did their best to make the unrelated grandchild their own. We have now learned from adopted people, birth parents and adopters that adoption is never a one-off event but remains a significant life factor that has to be acknowledged, respected and should be celebrated.

An adopted child will always be the child of two sets of parents. Most children adopted since the mid 1970s have been adopted

from the public care system and have suffered losses and traumas.
They come to adoption with both good and bad memories that
cannot be jettisoned at will. Some of their parents will have
neglected or abused them, but children can be attached to
neglectful and abusive parents. Adults, even those who were
adopted as infants, tell us that they grew up with a gap in their lives
that could not be filled until they found out more details about their
origins. Cutting off the past from the present and the future
confuses a child's sense of identity; adopted children, like all
children, need to understand where they came from and how they
got to where they are. Openness, not secrecy, is at the heart of
modern adoption. Adoptive grandparents can, helpfully, share some
of the responsibility for maintaining continuity for their adopted
grandchildren and for keeping them connected to their history.

Becoming related by adoption

While grandparents are increasingly finding a voice as workers,
consumers, voters, pensioners, caregivers, and significant relatives
of children in care, there is little recognition of the less conventional
role grandparents may or may not play when their own children
adopt. Becoming a grandparent, an aunt, an uncle or a cousin is
an automatic consequence when an infant is born. Most of us
can draw on experience and role models in the family to make a
reasonably good job of it. But it is not the same as becoming related
by adoption.

There are preparation and training courses for prospective adoptive
parents. Every applicant has to participate in a "home study", which
explores family networks and support systems. National Adoption
Standards make the provision of continuing adoption support for
the child, the adopters and the birth parents obligatory for every
agency. But as far as grandparents and other relatives are
concerned, although best social work practice will at least include
an interview with adoptive grandparents-to-be, this is not a
requirement and it is far from usual.

What then are grandparents to make of their children's plan to adopt? Are they expected to be as involved as they might be in the birth of a grandchild? Should they become as attached? As the awaited child is unlikely to be an infant, or there may be two or more children coming together, how will that affect existing family relationships? What happens if a child doesn't want to stay? Or if the prospective adopters find that they cannot cope and the placement disrupts? We have all heard funny stories about the small child who tells her mummy to send the new baby back to the shop when the novelty has worn off, but adopters may indeed decide to terminate the placement of a child. Can the grandparents and other relatives then remain in the picture? How do adoptive grandparents stand in relation to the birth grandparents and how many grandparents can one child have? What if the child is of a different culture, religion or ethnicity from the adopting family? What if "ready-made" children come with second marriages and are adopted by their step-parent – do the step-family's parents became step-grandparents? Or if adopting sons or daughters are gay or lesbian, do grandparents still count? And what if grandparents have their own life with no time to give?

This brief handbook aims to give grandparents-to-be and other relatives information about adoption today; it offers some facts about the children who need to be adopted and discusses how the wider family can support and be involved in building a family through adoption. Quotes are widely used to illustrate a point. Names and situations have been changed to preserve anonymity.

The stories of adopted children and their relatives are at the heart of the book. Chapter 9 describes how a family and their friends have got together to support the adoptive parents and their daughter.

Grandparents and other relatives come in many versions. Some are warm and friendly and others are more distant and formal. Some enjoy children and others find it harder to relate to them. Some are in and out of their children's homes and some are only seen once a year or live too far away to be seen at all. Very few grandmothers nowadays sit knitting in rose-covered cottages while grandfathers tell tales of bygone days in front of the fire. Grandparents, like their daughters and sons, work, travel, separate, divorce and re-marry. Adopted children have to find their way around a strange new family circle inhabited by unknown members and find a place in it for themselves. Grandparents and other relatives have an important role to play in making room for an adopted child in this circle.

istockphoto.com

What exactly is adoption?

I want to be adopted so I shall have a dad to give me away when I'm married.
Ten-year-old girl

Adoption is at least as old as the Bible. Moses was adopted by Pharaoh's daughter. The importance of continuity also seems to be an ancient issue, for Miriam, Moses' sister, smuggled their birth mother into the court to become his wet nurse. Although this was probably not an open adoption, because no one except Miriam and the infant Moses knew that the wet nurse was the mother, contact was maintained. This adoption also had other modern aspects: it was transracial, intercountry and the child was of a different religion.

Informal adoption has been a way of looking after children who cannot live with their birth family throughout known history. Stories about adopted children include *Oliver Twist*, by Charles Dickens, about the boy who was orphaned, who asked for more, and after great adversity was finally "adopted" by a single man who turned out to be his grandfather! And in *Daniel Deronda*, by George Elliot, Daniel was secretly "adopted" by another single, older man. He was lovingly brought up in an alien country and culture and spent much of his adult life searching for his roots and his identity.

Legal adoption in the UK was introduced in the second quarter of the 20th century and until the 1970s, it was largely regarded as a service for infertile couples. There were plenty of babies available before better birth control, acceptance of single parenthood and illegitimacy reduced the numbers drastically. The Adoption Acts of the late 1970s (in England & Wales and Scotland) made it clear that adoption was no longer to be a service for couples but a service for children who needed a new family. It became easier to dispense with the birth parents' agreement to adoption on grounds of consent being unreasonably withheld. From now on, the child's needs and rights were to be paramount. These needs and rights have since been further enshrined in successive legislation throughout the UK.

istockphoto.com

The adoption process

My daughter told us they were going to adopt.
Next thing we heard was, they were going to
adopt two together. Then they said they weren't
going to be babies. We didn't like to ask too much
but we didn't know what to expect or what was
expected of us.
Parents of adopters

George Bernard Shaw wrote in *Everybody's Political What's What:*

> *Parentage is a very important profession but no test for it is ever imposed in the interests of children.*

He might have added:

> *unless you are going to adopt.*

The adoption process can be stressful for people who are entering what can seem like a strange new world where no one can have children without being scrutinised – as they can in the real world – and where they will have to prove their competence to become parents.

At first we thought, 'What have we let ourselves in for?' But as it went on, we realised how much we had to learn.
Prospective adopters

The road to adoption may feel like a lonely journey and it is not always easy to ask for support from those who are nearest and dearest. There may be pain and embarrassment about infertility and the decision to adopt, and a fear of becoming "different". However, if members of the extended family know what is happening, what the process entails; if they can remain patient and encouraging without seeming intrusive, then adoption can, in time, become a very special family event.

I know my mum wanted me to tell her all about it but I couldn't. I felt too choked half the time. Also I didn't know if we'd get through and I didn't want to raise her hopes. But she was always there for me. She sort of encouraged me by just being around like normal and waiting till I was ready to talk.
Prospective adopter

The diagram below shows the adoption process from first enquiry to the Adoption Order for both family and child.

The adoption process (in England)

Adopters   **Child**

Contacting agencies and expressing an interest
Information meeting(s)
Registration of Interest
Stage One – pre-assessment
Police, health and other checks
Personal referees contacted
Some training and preparation
Stage Two – assessment
Further training and preparation
Work with an assessing social worker
Prospective Adopter's Report (PAR) completed
Adoption panel recommendation
Agency decision

Statutory looked after child review
Adoption plan agreed
To adoption panel if parents agree to adoption
Agency decision on the adoption plan
To court if parents do not agree to adoption
Care order and placement order
Family finding

Matching meeting and report
Adoption panel recommendation
Agency decision
Placement planning meeting
Possible child appreciation day
Introductions
Placement
Review of placement
Adoption application
Adoption Order

(Taken from *Adopting a Child* (Lord, 2013))

Initial information gathering

According to the latest government guidance for England, the process of adoption has to be completed in two stages. Scotland and Wales do not have equal requirements, but the content of the adoption process is the same.

Enquiry

- A single person or couple decide that they want to adopt a child or children.
- They approach their local authority or a voluntary adoption agency in their area for information.
- They will be given written information about adoption, the agency, the preparation and training offered and the statutory requirements regarding health, police checks and personal references. This information should be available in the main languages spoken in the locality.
- They will be invited to an Open Meeting held regularly for all enquirers, followed by a one-off consultation with a social worker to learn about the kinds of children needing new families.

This is a good opportunity for relatives to be involved. Although they may not always suggest it, nearly all agencies would welcome first-time enquirers to bring friends or relations to an initial meeting. And there is never any harm in asking! It is especially important for prospective single adopters to bring someone they can talk with after the meeting.

If the prospective adopters decide to proceed, they will be asked to complete a "Registration of Interest" form.

Stage One

At this stage, the agency will offer applicants some initial training and preparation. Also, because children must be protected, all prospective adopters have to agree to health, police and social services checks. References will then be followed up. **Adopters are asked to give the names of personal referees, who know them well and are not related, but relatives can be named as additional referees; this offers an easy way of including them in the process.**

Applicants will be given every opportunity to withdraw at this point. Adoption is not for everyone.

Stage One should take no longer than two months to complete.

Stage Two

Home study

This is the very personal and searching part of the process. It is not an assessment of the accommodation, as is sometimes thought. If families feel comfortable in their homes, and as long as the physical surroundings don't pose a risk for a child, it is likely a child would also be comfortable. Standards of housekeeping should not be on trial and no one should feel the need to tidy up before the social worker arrives.

A social worker will visit the home several times to gather evidence of the applicants' competence and capacity to become parents by adoption. During this time, the prospective adopters may feel that their whole lives are under public scrutiny and that their privacy and dignity are under attack. In these circumstances, it is not surprising if they withdraw from further discussion with members of their own family.

I was expected to talk about things I never think about. I suppose to begin with I was resentful really. Looking back it made me understand better about me as a child and what it would be like for

*a child having me as a dad. But my family thought
it was just social workers being nosy and so I never
really talked to them about it. They never really
caught on about adoption.*
Prospective adopter

The home study will include an assessment of:

- family histories, lifestyles and aspirations in relation to adoption;
- parenting experience and experience of being parented;
- reasons for childlessness and attitudes to infertility or wanting more children by adoption;
- relationship with partner, if applicable, and previous long-term relationships;
- support from the extended family, friends and community;
- ethnicity, culture and religious practice;
- attitude to openness towards the birth family and attitude regarding continuity for the child;
- ability to ask for help and work with agencies;
- employment, education and finance.

**Relatives should be interviewed during this phase if they
have been named as referees or if they will be expected to
make a significant contribution to the placement.**

---

*I told them from the start that my sister would look
after him from school till I come home. She lives
near and she's got two of her own and she doesn't
work and she offered. I can't afford to lose my job.
My social worker saw as much of my sister and her
husband as of me. I began to wonder 'who's going
to adopt?' But it's worked out all right and Jake's
got two new families for the price of one.*
Single parent adopter

Training

All adoption agencies have to provide preparation and training for prospective adopters. Groups of several couples and single people usually meet weekly for about six sessions, or the agency may offer intensive whole days at weekends over a shorter period. Some agencies encourage single adopters to bring a relative or friend to the training sessions. Only a handful of agencies offer specific training to grandparents and other relatives.

The training for prospective adopters will include:

- learning about how children become attached to their carers and how attachments can become disturbed;
- issues of loss, separation and trauma;
- the significance of continuity, connection and contact for children who cannot live with their birth parents;
- why children need to be adopted and why families adopt;
- the experiences of families that have adopted;
- the meaning of family histories, systems and stories;
- health and education;
- the importance of a supportive network;
- anti-discriminatory practice in the family and the community.

It is helpful if family members know what is being covered in the training. Showing an interest in the written course material may lead to easier communication about the adoption plan.

At the end of the home study and training, the social worker and applicants will write a report, called the Prospective Adopter's Report (PAR) together for the agency's Adoption Panel. This panel, made up of professionals and lay people experienced in adoption, will recommend whether the applicants should be approved as prospective parents. Panels will invite the applicants to come and meet the members of the panel with their social worker when their application is discussed. If the applicants are not approved, the agency must give them information about why their application has been turned down and how to appeal against the decision. It can be hard for parents-in-waiting to have to ask for "public approval" to start a family.

We know social services have to look after the children in the first place, but going to panel made us feel even more different from the rest of the family. These strangers have to read everything there is to know about you before they can approve you. And even with our social worker saying it would be all right, we were in a state for the three weeks leading up to it and on the day we were so nervous we were both sick. You can't explain to people who've had their own children, how it feels for your whole future to depend on an official decision.
Adoptive parent

Matching and preparation for a specific child or children

During the whole process so far, prospective adopters will have been thinking about the child or children they might adopt. They may already have identified a child from one of several photo-listing publications that feature profiles and photographs of children who need new families. These children will have gone through their own part of the adoption process (see diagram) and will be ready to be "matched" with a family.

There is no knowing for sure which child should be placed in which family; surprising matches have been made and have worked out well. By the time prospective adopters have been approved, they will probably feel more confident about discussing possible children with family members. But beware about influencing their choice! It is rather like choosing a partner for life and chemistry must be allowed to play its part. On the whole, it is more helpful to encourage adopters to ask the right questions about a child who appeals to them, than to try to get them to make the right choice. If they are given all the information available about a child, they will be able to make an informed decision about whether they and the child should be "matched".

The most important element of the matching process is the preparation for having a specific child. How will this child fit into this family? Lack of information at this stage can cause the adoption to break down later. Adopters need every bit of available information to help them to decide whether they are the right family for a particular child. A good agency will organise a Child Appreciation Day to ensure that adopters have the opportunity to meet everyone who knows the child: present and previous carers, social workers, teachers, medical practitioners, health visitors and therapists. They should also have the opportunity to meet the birth family if at all possible. They or their worker should be told all the known facts including the painful ones. They should have access to the child's files and they should be given a record of all the child's moves, separations and losses.

This can be an overwhelming time for adopters and interest from their parents, other relatives and friends is usually appreciated, although there will be a fitting reluctance to share intimate details about a child and the birth parents when the child is not yet theirs. If information about a child is not forthcoming, a little prodding and support from relatives to give the prospective adopters the confidence to ask for what should be theirs by right, would not come amiss. Grandparents could offer to meet the child's birth grandparents at this point; in some cases where this has happened, a relatively stress-free route for communication has been established between the two families.

It may become necessary for the prospective adopters to withdraw if they discover that they would, after all, not be the right parents for this child. If they do, they will need all the support they can get because they may feel they are failing a child who needs them. But better by far to enable people to find out what they can and what they can't do now, than to encourage them to persevere with a placement that could easily disrupt. The Stage Two assessment should take no longer than four months.

My brother and sister-in-law went ahead with the two boys; they didn't ask us and we didn't say

*anything but we knew it wasn't right. That older
boy's problems were way beyond what they would
be able to cope with. In the end, they found out
for themselves so we could just prop them up
without interfering.*
Brother of prospective adopters

Introduction and placement

Introductions are as long or as short as a piece of string. Everything
will depend on the child's need and capacity to become familiar and
comfortable with new people and new places. It has to be
remembered that every move for the child, however positive, also
means a separation from other familiar people and places.

Very often adopters regard introductions as private and personal
and there may be a virtual "keep out" notice as far as the extended
family is concerned.

---

*I was ready to welcome this little girl into the
family, just as I've welcomed all my other
grandchildren but my son didn't give me a chance.
She'd moved in before I met her and I don't think
we ever got off on the right foot after that. She
saw me as someone intruding instead of someone
belonging.*
Grandmother of a six-year-old adopted girl

---

*I dreaded my mum coming round. She goes over
the top and I was afraid she'd cluck all over them
or ask them things or expect them to come and sit
on her lap. In the end I talked to her about it and
she was great. The children took to her straight
away; they moved in for her as much as for us!
And now she's the gran they never had.*
Adoptive parent of sibling group

When children move in to a new home with new parents there is often a honeymoon period before life resumes as normal. And normal can range from the usual ups and downs of living with children to more downs and less ups than we are used to in ordinary family life.

This is the time when grandparents and other relatives can rally round to offer practical help while avoiding criticism of the children or of the parent's handling of the children. Babysitting, outings, washing and ironing, gardening, cooking a meal and giving lifts will be seen as more supportive than giving advice. And it is never helpful to tell adopters who are struggling with unusual situations that they are not unusual or that the children will settle down soon. On the other hand, a good listener to tales of many woes, but also of small triumphs, is mostly very welcome.

Dad isn't fussed about what the children do or don't do. He gets on with all the odd jobs around the house and he lets them help. If they mess up he'll tell them, not get on at them. Then he'll sit down and make a cup of tea and I tell him all the latest. He won't say much, but he listens and he nods and looks pleased when he hears about a little bit of progress one of them has made.
Single adoptive parent of two brothers

Until an Adoption Order is made, there will be regular reviews of the placement. They are a safeguard for the child but also an opportunity for the new family to get the support and advice they need. **Grandparents and other relatives should be welcome.**

Adoption and post-adoption
The final step of the adoption process is the making of an Adoption Order in Court. Some adoptions go ahead pretty quickly, others are delayed for a variety of reasons: the child is not ready, the parents are not confident enough to proceed, the birth parents are contesting the

application, the social workers have not completed the paperwork, a document is missing or the Court is dealing with a backlog.

The child has to have been in placement for a specific time before an application for an Order can be made. An Adoption Order can be granted up to the day a child reaches the age of 18.

Sometimes an Adoption Order can reassure a child and calm a turbulent passage; or it can make a seemingly settled child feel secure enough to open the floodgates and let rip; or it can simply be a happy event in a family story. In any case, it is a cause for a family celebration that can be added to the rest of the annual rituals.

The adoption process ends with the Order but adoption will be a lifetime factor for the child and all the family members. This has long been recognised by adoption practitioners and has now been acknowledged by the policy makers. All adoption agencies have a duty to assess the adoption support needs of families, including financial support, and to make a plan accordingly. Schools also have an obligation and a budget to meet special educational needs of adopted children. The term "adoption support" covers all the services required before and after an Order is made. The help that grandparents and other relatives can offer will be taken into account when adoption support plans are agreed.

We couldn't have done without all the help the agency gave us right up to the time she was 18. And then they kept in touch and helped out when we had problems with benefits and wheelchairs and things because they knew her and the adult disability team in our area didn't understand about adoption. But the best were my mum and dad. They were always there for us. They never complained about having a severely disabled grandchild. They love her, like we do, and you can't buy that.
Adopter of young person with multiple impairments

03

Some legal points

- Grandparents and other relatives have no legal rights regarding adopted or birth children of the family.
- Grandparents and other relatives can be named as guardians for an adopted child (or birth child) by the adoptive parents in their wills.
- Adopted children have the same inheritance rights as children born to the family.
- Adopted children have exactly the same legal status as children born to the family.
- If an adoption disrupts after an order is made, the child remains the legal child of the adoptive parents, unless another family adopts the child.
- If an adopted child comes into public care, the adopters retain parental responsibility. According to UK legislation and/or guidance, relatives and significant others have to be considered as carers before a child is placed outside the family network.
- It is usual for adopted children to take the adopters' family name, but it is not a requirement. Older children sometimes prefer to keep their names or to add the adopters' name to their own.
- An adopted child does not retain a legal connection to their birth parents.

- An adopted person living in England, Wales or Northern Ireland has the right to identifying information about their birth family when they are 18. In Scotland, the age is 16.
- Legislation in the UK allows two single people, of the same or different sex, to adopt together if they are in an established relationship.
- Under adoption legislation in England and Wales and Northern Ireland, birth parents have the right to approach specified agencies for information about their adopted child when that child reaches the age of 18. In Scotland there is no such legal right, but birth parents can request and receive a similar service.

04

Who are
the children?

*I knew there weren't enough babies to go round,
but I never knew there were so many children
waiting to be adopted.*
Adoptive grandparent of three sisters

Children, like families, come in all shapes and sizes and every child is unique. That is why it is not possible to say what kind of child parents will adopt; there is no "kind of child". An eight-year-old could have the emotional age of a toddler and the intellectual ability of a child of ten.

Tanya, aged seven, followed her new mum everywhere including the toilet and would not be left alone for a moment. Bedtime was agony for her because she was afraid that as soon as she fell asleep, she would be abandoned. Whenever she woke up in the night, she crept into her new parents' bed. Although she hated to leave her mother to go to school, she was easily top of the class and had a reading age of 12.

The few healthy babies who need to be adopted are usually placed with young childless couples, but there are not enough babies to go around. Some people, who only want very young children, adopt them from overseas, but this is an expensive and uncertain business. It is also the case that many more of the poorer nations are striving to keep their children in their own country while, at the same time, the law regarding adoption of children from overseas has become more stringent in the UK.

Most of the children who need new families today have been taken away from their birth parents. They come from all ethnic backgrounds and may have a mixed heritage. They may have been neglected or rejected; they may have parents who are too sick to care for them; they may have been emotionally, physically or sexually abused by members of their own family or their family may have been unable to protect them from abuse by others. Many of these children are part of a sibling group; some have mild to severe disabilities or learning difficulties, and some have been diagnosed with behavioural difficulties like ADHD (attention deficit hyperactivity disorder) or with an attachment disorder (a damaged capacity to make meaningful relationships due to earlier experiences). At some point, a court will have decided that these children would be at risk of significant harm if they returned to their homes. Nearly all of them will have been living with foster families and many of them will have moved several times while in foster care.

Children who have been born with a physical, sensory or intellectual impairment may need new families because their parents are not able to cope with disability or, in rare cases, they may even have caused the impairment. Bringing a disabled child into a family creates a special kind of adoption. Parents have to want that child because of, and not in spite of, the impairment. Disabled children must never be regarded as second best but they do need a family that will fight for their rights, for their benefits, for their education and health care, for their social inclusion and for their transition to independence. Enough to keep the whole extended family busy!

Never lose sight of the child

It is possible to get carried away by trying to be honest about the children who need new families, but by focusing on their pain and problems, we may lose sight of the individual child. Like all children, these are also chatty, giggly, generous, gentle, funny, kind, quick or slow, robust, resilient, energetic and, above all, brave children. They have possibly faced up to more hurt and disappointment than most of us have to deal with in a lifetime. It is important for everyone in the family to understand something about the history of children who are adopted from care, but it is also important to respect the new parents' concern about protecting their new child. It isn't necessary for relations to know every single detail from the very beginning in order to feel related.

We didn't exactly hide anything about Liam, we gave my parents the general idea, but we didn't go into the gory details. We thought it would best come out when he was ready to talk about it himself. And he did – once he got used to his new Nanna, he told her things even we didn't know. It was a good job she was prepared for it or it would have knocked her sideways.
Adopter of four-year-old boy

It has to be self-evident that children who have had a hard time are not going to be easy to bring up. They will need patience and a great deal of consistent care and attention before they can learn to trust their new family and the world around them. This new world will include not only parents, but grandparents, uncles, aunts, cousins and a medley of other relatives.

We would like a child joining a new family to be able to say with Miranda from Shakespeare's *The Tempest:*

> *O, wonder!*
> *How many goodly creatures are there here!*
> *How beauteous mankind is! O brave new world*
> *That has such people in't! (Act 5 Scene 1)*

Family systems
and circles

*I've got an old Nan and a new Gran but I don't
know how to fit them together.*
Adopted boy aged seven

Every family tells a story. Or several stories, or the same story from different perspectives. We grow up with our family stories; we grow up learning slowly who all the characters are: who is who in the family circle. Some members of this circle may never be seen by the child growing up, but if they appear in the family stories, they will nevertheless be known as "Uncle Harry with the large ears" or "cousin Midge who happens to be very tall".

Holding collective memories

Grandparents and other older relatives are usually the main storytellers in the family. They hold the collective memories. In some cultures where there is a strong oral tradition, the elders of the tribe are revered because they alone pass on the history of the family, the community and the nation. Hence there is a deep respect for old age and the wisdom of experience. In Western societies there is no such built-in respect for elders – the elders have to earn it. They must be tactful, may not interfere, be available when needed, avoid giving advice but be ready to share what they have learned. If they tell their stories too often, someone will soon say: 'Oh Grandma, you've told us that a dozen times'. Nevertheless, most families value their stories; they return to them again and again and build on them as they go along.

Entering the family circle

How will a child enter the family circle and catch up with the stories? New parents may be too busy with the many aspects of the parenting-by-adoption task to fill the child in with what other children learn from the cradle. They might welcome an offer of help from grandparents or other relatives – as long as they are kept in the picture.

A new child in the family could perhaps spend one afternoon a week with older relations for the express purpose of introducing the child to the family circle and family stories. Old family photographs are good triggers for storytelling; mementoes can be shared with the child and treasures can be exhibited on these special occasions: a school report, a certificate for an achievement, a card made for an anniversary long ago, a milk tooth or a lock of baby hair preserved, a remembrance of a loved pet, a medal belonging to an uncle killed in a war. Not all memories have to be happy ones. The child is joining a real family, not a fairy tale.

Listening to new family stories and being absorbed into a new family circle should give children the opportunity to share some of their own stories and to make connections between the two. If children can acknowledge where they have come from, and learn to value the good bits of their past, then they will be able to concentrate better on their new family. There's a lot of catching up to do when children are adopted – the child has to catch up with the family and the family has to catch up with the years the child was elsewhere. Grandparents and other relatives have an essential inter-generational role to play.

I fetched her from school on Thursdays and she came to my place. We made a ritual out of it. First there was milk and a different cake I made for her every week. She liked to know about baking so we wrote the recipes out together and pasted them into a folder that she kept in my kitchen with my cookery books. Then it was the family albums. She always remembered where we'd left off the last time but more often than not she wanted to go back a bit or start again from the beginning. Sometimes she asked that many questions, it set me off on memory lane, so we only had time to look at a couple of pages before it was time to take her home.

Grandparent of an adopted ten-year-old girl

Every family is different

There is yet more to accomplish for the child entering the new family circle. Every family has its own lifestyle, its own system, as well as its own stories. No one family has quite the same way as any other of dealing with health, education, work, money, travel, discipline, noise, cleanliness, order, food, leisure, illness, hospitality and everything else that makes them who they are. The value put on healthy eating, for instance, the rules about sitting up at the table or the rituals for making mealtimes shared occasions for exchanging the news of the day, will vary tremendously between families.

Tracy had mostly chips in paper bags with her birth mum. Her foster carer was very strict about eating at regular times sitting up at the table with the other children. Now she can't figure out how to handle our more casual style of eating together, on our laps, at different times to suit the working members of the family. She goes frantic if a meal is late; she always wants to know what the rules are even when there aren't any.
Adopter of a six-year-old girl

And this is only one aspect of dozens that may be confusing Tracy about her new family's system. Even the meaning of well-known words may become obscure. What does this family mean by "keeping in touch" for example? Does it mean talking on the phone daily, keeping an "open house" for family members, friends and neighbours, visiting by invitation only, sending birthday cards, writing letters and emails, or is contact restricted to family celebrations and times of crisis? When they meet, do they hug, kiss, shake hands or avoid physical contact?

And, most relevant for grandparents and other older relatives, how do the generations interact? How do the branches of the family tree hold together? Children who come from dysfunctional families will have to learn how this one functions properly, that some branches of the tree are more frail than others but that they will survive because the tree is strong. Grandparents and other relatives are important players in this new system and can help to guide the new child through what may seem to be an incomprehensible maze of values, standards and behaviours.

Continuity, connection and contact

A ten-year-old boy became devoted to the postman because it was he who brought letters from his brothers and sisters.

It used to be thought that adoption was a neat solution for the birth mother who couldn't look after her child, for the child who needed a family and for the childless adopters. All three parties to adoption could make a clean start and forget all about the birth, the rejection and the infertility. Over the years, we have learned, from the people themselves, that those who have been adopted need to know who they are and why they are where they are, that adopters have to negotiate and celebrate a different way of building a family and that birth mothers never forget. There may be momentous changes, like adoption, but there are no fresh starts in life: we can only begin life once and finish it once and we have to make the most of the bit in between; we have to carry our baggage and create a whole life by remaining connected to both ends. We can't live a healthy life in pieces. "She's gone to pieces" is an accurate description of someone who can't hold their life together. Anything we try to cut out of our story has a habit of hitting back at us. But this doesn't mean that children can't let go of their fears and get on with their new life.

We thought it best to let bygones be bygones and we agreed we'd never talk about his dad to our adopted son unless he brought it up himself. Danny was scared of him, we knew that, but he was going to be in prison for years. It was all in the past and Danny knew he was safe with us.

It wasn't until Danny had been with us for a year that he started having these terrible nightmares. He was dreaming about this big animal climbing up the drainpipe and getting him – he'd wake up screaming. From things he said, we thought he was having nightmares about his dad coming to get him. So we started to talk about what had happened to him. How we wouldn't let anyone hurt him but how we couldn't take away the hurt his dad had done. We told him that he didn't have to worry about it happening again and he didn't have to pretend it never happened.

After a bit he calmed down and the nightmares stopped gradually. Then one day he said, 'I think about my dad a lot but I'm not scared any more. When I'm bigger I'd like to go and see if he's OK.'
Adopters of an eight-year-old boy

We sometimes talk about going back to our roots; plants have roots, people have legs and can move. Children can move to new families without lasting damage but the transition has to be managed without breaking the thread of continuity with the past and the connection to their birth family.

The need for connection

Children's need for connection and continuity may, or may not, lead to contact with the birth family after they are placed for adoption. And contact can range from face-to-face visits arranged by the two families themselves to an annual exchange of news through a third party – usually the adoption agency that arranged the placement. Contact may have to be supervised by social workers to protect the child and the adopters should be aware of what is said on the telephone, in text messages, emails and on social networking websites. This becomes more difficult when children are teenagers and is a good example of how adoption can make a difference to family life. Unsupervised internet use could lead to unplanned contact between adopted children and their birth families (for more information, see *Facing up to Facebook* (Fursland, 2013)).

If contact is deemed to be unsafe or undesirable for children, there are ways of keeping absent people in mind that do not pose a danger.

Ruby, aged 12, and her sister Jade, aged ten, had frightening memories of their mother who was a long-term patient in a psychiatric hospital. They visited her once with their adoptive parents and were distressed because she didn't recognise them. They were also relieved to see that she was being looked after at last. Ruby told her mother's social worker, 'We don't have to see her because our new mum's put our old mum in the family circle, so we won't lose her'.

Contact plans

A plan for contact with the birth family has to be considered for every child placed for adoption. The purpose of contact has to be clear and the plan has to be in the child's interests. Questions of where, when, how often and with whom, should be negotiated with the adopters. And it is always important to hear the views of the children – only they can tell us about their most meaningful connections. Very often they will include current and past carers who may have played as significant a part in their lives as their birth family.

It is a mistake to think that children need to "settle" in the adoptive home before they have any contact with people from their past life. On the contrary, they will settle more easily and be more confident if the links are preserved from the beginning. Imagine getting married and being told that in order to make the marriage work, you may not hear or see any of your other loved ones for three months at least! You could blame and resent your new partner for imposing such conditions!

At best, contact with birth relatives and other significant people is like seeing members of your extended family – you like some more than others – sometimes family occasions work and sometimes they don't – but that's families for you. At worst, there can be conflict and then outside help should be available to mediate and negotiate more acceptable contact arrangements. Sometimes children are upset before and after meetings and this has been used as a reason for terminating contact. It may be that there are specific reasons for the upset, which should be explored, or it may be that children need more preparation and more support, but very rarely is it an indication for contact to stop. We must allow children to feel sad and to be upset; they can't be happy all the time.

Where do grandparents and other relatives come in to these contact arrangements?

Perhaps they are well placed to take some of the heat out of the event. Contact can be a stressful experience for both families as well as for the child and, as in other family situations, the presence of less intensely involved members of the family can be a calming and supportive influence.

When it was time for one of those contact meetings, we always made a family occasion of it. We'd plan a picnic or some kind of outing and it would be the children and my daughter and son-in-law and me; Beryl (birth mother) would bring her mother along and that made it easier for the children; it opened it out more somehow and they could see that we all got on together. Their granny was a nice woman but very shy. The children really liked seeing her but I don't think she'd have come if I hadn't been there. The younger one said to us at one contact meeting, 'How many grannies am I allowed to have?'
Grandparent of three

Ethnicity, religion and culture

They're not really the same as me but they're not really different.
Eight-year-old African-Caribbean child adopted by black mixed heritage parents

If you had to describe yourself, long distance, to an alien on another planet, what would you say? What is important about the way you look, move, behave, dress, eat and sleep? Do your own family, the community you belong to, the language you speak and the country you live in have some bearing on who you are? Are your beliefs and values, the way you feel and relate to others, also part of you? How will you convey what you mean? If you tell the alien that you are white or black, will he understand that white means anything from pink to beige and black means anything from olive to dark brown?

Although new families are not "aliens from another planet", children joining a new family can feel bemused or puzzled by an unfamiliar culture or religious practice and, if the family is of a different ethnicity to their own, may find it hard to explain themselves or to hold on to their own picture of themselves. It is therefore the aim of adoption agencies to match the child with adopters who will be able to help the child to understand and appreciate their background and culture. We have learned how vital it is for children's sense of identity and self-esteem to grow up in families that can embrace and, where possible, share their cultural, religious and ethnic heritage. Where the adoptive family does not "match" all the child's characteristics, there is an expectation that support will be available to both the family and the child.

Even if a child comes from exactly the same minority ethnic background as the adopters, the two mothers might come from different communities or tribes or sects or castes from within the same country. The fathers might vary from pale to dark of the same skin colour. Then there is religion: a Protestant Christian from Cheltenham is not the same as a Protestant Christian from Northern Ireland. There are many accepted versions of each of the major religions and there are less well-known alternative faiths. Class and culture can be even more confusing: Does it matter how we speak? What do we read or watch on television? Which sport do we play or follow? Do we live for the day or plan for tomorrow?

They're not too bad but they speak posh, they don't watch Big Brother, they don't know nothing about football and we're always having to go to the library. Then they make me save half my pocket money. I don't know why. But I like them 'cause they're nice. And there's all the aunts and uncles and grandma and that – they're all like that – but they're nice too.
Black child adopted by black family

What can grandparents do?

So how can grandparents and other relatives help adopted children to strengthen their own identities? To appreciate similarities and also acknowledge that they are different from new family members? Never suggest that differences don't matter or will not be noticed – that could make a child feel insignificant or even invisible. It is better to talk about the difference and to find a way to celebrate it.

Grandpa Ron and me used to make a point of telling Josie how much we admired her hair. I took a course on how to braid Afro hair and then we used to spend hours trying out different styles. It really takes hours and I think my daughter-in-law was pleased I could do it because she works and doesn't have the time – although she's African and we're not. Josie was ten when she came to us and she's 14 now but she still comes to me to have her hair done. It gives us a closeness we wouldn't have had otherwise. Grandpa Ron always comes to look when we've finished and she loves it when he

approves. He takes photos to keep a record of all
the different styles.
Adoptive grandparent

Other relatives may like to become experts on the various festivals
and rituals to which the child has been accustomed and help to
provide the right food and venue at the right time to celebrate as
a family.

At one time we only had family get togethers at
Christmas and birthdays but now we have
adoption days and Chinese New Year as well. I
make the jiaozi (New Year dumplings) and get all
the bits and pieces like chocolate money stuffed in
red envelopes and I decorate the house with
special Chinese banners. To begin with it was more
for my adopted nieces, but now we're all getting
more interested in their background and we're all
kind of discovering about it together.
Adoptive aunt

There are as many ways of communicating with children about who
they are, as there are ways of describing ourselves to aliens. Some
ways will work better than others, but the important thing is to take
every opportunity to keep on trying.

08

Common problems, questions and some answers

Can I be a real grandparent to unrelated children – will I be able to love them?

It is natural and usual for grandparents to love their grandchildren. They won't necessarily love them all the same and they may not live close to them but, on the whole, they often enjoy a special relationship with their grandchildren, partly because they don't have the responsibility of bringing them up. Unless they offer regular childcare to enable their own children to work, grandparents can spoil their children and "hand them back" when they've had enough! Grandchildren bring renewal to the whole family; their birth signals hope for the future and for the survival of the tribe. Of course, a great part of the pleasure they give to the family has to do with watching their development from babyhood: 'hasn't he grown?' or 'she's always been a smiler', and with their likeness to someone else: 'you are the image of your mother at the same age' or: 'just like your father – can't wait for anything'. But how will it be if the adopted child is older or disabled, troubled by past events and has a different genetic heritage handed down from another family? And how about being faced with two, three or even more sisters and brothers one by one or even all at the same time?

*It was hard for my mother to accept the idea of
our adopting disabled children. But once she got
over the initial shock, she grew very fond of them
and used to call Robert and Claude 'my boys'. She
was anxious for us the first time and the second,
but by the time we took Corena she'd given up
worrying. She'd always said that she didn't want
her grandchildren to call her "nanna" – she wanted
to be "gran" or "grandma" – but they all called her
"nanna" and she liked it.*
Adoptive parent in *Whatever Happened to Adam?*
BAAF, 1998

It is not always easy for grandparents to accept their adult children's
infertility. Their feelings of disappointment and their sense of loss
and discontinuation often remain unacknowledged because they are
not the main players in the adoption scenario.

*Betsy was adopted. For her eighth birthday, she
and her mother had decided to make Betsy's room
into a big girl's room. They chose wallpaper and
paint and fabric for curtains and did the whole
room by themselves. They had great fun and were
both excited and pleased with the result. The
grandparents were there for Betsy's birthday
dinner. After the cake, Betsy and her mother each
took one of Nana's hands and told her to close her
eyes and they would lead her to a surprise. They
walked her down the hallway to the bedroom door
and told her to open her eyes. She did. She looked
around the room and finally said, 'What a beautiful
room for someone else's child'.*
(From *The Family of Adoption* by Joyce Maguire
Pavo, Boston: Beacon Press, 1998)

I don't suppose this grandmother meant to be so terribly unkind.
She was probably even unaware of her sadness that Betsy was not
her genetic grandchild. She may have been a perfectly caring and
loving grandmother for most of the time. But being aware about
adoption issues and feelings that may recur is essential to the wellbeing of the adoptive family.

*My daughter has adopted five children so I'm their
adoptive grandmother. I think you can learn to be
an adoptive grandparent but it's not the same as
when I had my two children and their nannas were
there from the beginning – right there in the
hospital and it just grew from that. If your adult
children adopt a baby it could be the same but not
if they come older. You have to fit in more with
what they need. I've been upset – very, very upset
– when there have been real problems but you
can't interfere. You've got to be there for them but
you mustn't expect too much.*
Nanna by adoption in *Be My Parent*, April 1999

Some adopted children may avoid close relationships with new
parents to begin with and find it easier to relate to a comfortable
old grandparent, a more distant aunt or an accepting new cousin,
preferably one at a time. Other children will cope best in the hurly
burly of a large, open family where everybody comes and goes and
they can get by without being noticed too much. If grandparents
and other relatives can "fit in more with what they need", there is a
good chance that love will grow in time. And if not love, then
respect and concern for a young person who has lost one family
and is brave enough to risk having another. It may never feel the
same as having related grandchildren, nieces, nephews or cousins,
but the difference can be enriching and lead to a wider appreciation
of the family circle.

Will an older child learn to love their new family?

Children can love many adults, especially if the adults respect each other and tell the same story. We have learnt from divorce that it is more difficult for children to maintain positive emotional ties with adults who are hostile to each other.

It used to be thought that children could transfer their attachments from one group of people to another and that we had to help them to detach from their birth families or previous carers before they could attach to adopters. But this doesn't make sense. In real life we don't have to jettison an old friend before we make a new one. Nor do we lose our own family when we become a member of our partner's family. As the saying goes: 'You're not losing a daughter but gaining a son'. In fact, from infancy on we learn to extend our attachments, not to exchange one for another. Healthy infants extend their attachments from their main carer to the rest of the family and, step-by-step, to significant people in the outside world. It is a process of building more relationships, not of weeding them out. Children who have been in the care system have already sustained losses and we must help them to retain as many of their previous relationships as is compatible with their safety and wellbeing.

It is then not a matter of changing from the old to the new, but of changing the balance between the old and the new. Picture a seesaw. At the beginning of the road to adoption, the weight is with the birth family and/or previous carers while the adopters are up in the air. The child starts off where the weight is and gradually has to work her or his way towards the adopters so that the weight will shift to them and their end of the seesaw will touch the ground. It is a difficult journey and often there are obstacles to negotiate. There is usually a spurt to begin with (known as the "honeymoon"), until the child reaches the middle of the seesaw where she or he is likely to get stuck for a bit with both families hovering at the same level on either side. At this point it may look as though the child is battling to keep control of the seesaw and perhaps would like to say: 'Hold on to me – don't let me go'. If the child is safely held, the slow move towards investing wholeheartedly in the new family can follow.

What are the obstacles some adopted children face?

Disordered attachments
Attachments become disordered if children are hurt, neglected, rejected or abandoned by the very people who should be caring for them. Instead of healthy attachments that can be extended, these children tend to form insecure attachments that lead to difficulties in making new relationships. They may make excessive demands on the one hand or avoid any form of closeness on the other. They have no safe pattern to follow.

It was like Jonathan wasn't really with us. He was living in the house and he wasn't much trouble but he kept us at a distance. It was bad enough for us, we'd been warned to expect it, but my mother kept trying to draw him out and getting hurt by what he said to her. He told her to shut up because she wasn't his real grandma. We had to explain to her why he was like that. I think it took nearly a year before he could respond and then it was only for some of the time with some people. Adopter of ten-year-old boy, Jonathan

---

I was hurt when Jonathan said I wasn't his real grandma, but when my son explained about him I could see that I wasn't as hurt as he had been. Jonathan's grandmother

---

If the grandmother had been included in the preparation, she might have been able to support the parents through a particularly stressful period.

Lack of trust

Children who have been repeatedly let down by adults are not trusting. They cannot take it for granted that they will not be let down again and it may be easier for them not to risk it. Building their trust in the new family is a major task in which all family members can participate. Small things matter: making promises and keeping them, always turning up at the school gates on time, keeping confidences, hearing what the child says, respecting the child and their new parents, remembering birthdays and anniversaries, being consistent about praise and discipline and being available.

I remember I was really rude to my grandma when I was first adopted. She kept on and on at me to talk to her and she really got on my nerves. But she went on coming to see me and brought me things even when I was rude, and now we're really good friends because I know I can trust her.
Jonathan, aged 12

Unfinished business

If children are moved into an adoptive placement without enough preparation, they will arrive confused and unable to make the transition without becoming disturbed and creating disturbance. They will be trying to deal with "unfinished business". If they have had to say "goodbye" to their birth family, they may blame the adopters for asking the impossible. If they have had to leave a loved foster family too abruptly, the loss could outweigh gaining a new family. If they have been separated from brothers and sisters, they may be preoccupied with becoming reunited. If they do not know or cannot make sense of their own story, they will not make sense of their new situation. There is no substitute for adequate preparation for children – and the same is true for adopters – but sometimes the new family has to do this work in retrospect, as well as they can. Whatever the age and understanding of a child, ways can be found to communicate and to explore together, the road the child has travelled to be adopted.

Auntie Annie was always making things for all the children in the family. When Alison, aged five, was adopted, she seemed not to understand what was happening to her. She repeatedly asked for her previous carers. Auntie Annie made paper dolls to represent all the people Alison had lived with. She got Alison to describe them and to decide what clothes they should wear. Then she made a special box for the dolls where they could be safe. Alison seemed to be totally preoccupied with these dolls and wouldn't play with any of the other toys the adopters had prepared for her. She talked to the dolls and slept with them under her pillow. After a few days, Auntie Annie added dolls to represent Alison's new family and made a second special box for them. To begin with, Alison wouldn't play with the new dolls. Then she slowly included them one at a time in her games until they were all mixed up together and living in the same box. She used the other box for their spare clothes that Auntie Annie kept on supplying to order. Only much later did Alison start playing with other toys.

Every child placed for adoption should have a life story book – a record, with photographs, drawings and maps of each person and place and event that have featured in their life so far. Life story books can be shared and read over and over again with additional explanations, and they can be updated to include the present and to draw the child's life into a continuous whole. That is the ideal! Unfortunately, not all life story books are complete or comprehensive; many avoid the painful bits of the story and some are no more than photograph albums. But it is never too late to augment a life story book or even to begin a new one. *My Life and Me* and *Me and My Family*, (by Jean Camis/Jean Maye, published by BAAF, 2001 and 2011) are useful tools to get going with some simple, interactive ideas.

Children may feel reluctant about sharing their life story with members of their new family but, in due course, it will be reassuring and confirming for them to know that not only parents, but also other relatives have included their story in the family history.

"Into moves"

Some children have been moved so often that moving itself becomes the name of the game. You never have to make the best or the most of anything because there will be another move soon. And moves are exciting because you never know what you will find and the grass just might be greener next time. These children have no concept of permanence and usually move without a backward glance. People mistakenly think that they have settled quickly because the move has been painless, but in truth, children who are "into moves" see themselves as merely passing through.

On the day she moved to her adoption placement, seven-year-old Leila said to her social worker: 'Next time I'd like a family by the seaside'.

The intended permanence of adoption has to be demonstrated and emphasised continuously. All the family members can help: talking about events in the future, planning future holidays together, looking ahead to family celebrations, discussing choices in education, making long-term arrangements for health care and buying winter clothes in the summer or vice versa will all contribute to giving children a sense of staying where they are.

How will the child fit in with existing grandchildren, nephews and nieces?

Generally children will accept half-siblings, stepsiblings and adopted siblings if the parents and the rest of the family are comfortable with the situation. The same applies to grandchildren, nephews and nieces. There may be rivalry and jealousy but this also happens in the most regular and best-regulated families. It is no good pretending that love will be instant or that the new arrival will have an equal share of it from the word go. In any case, there are no equal shares of love. But the idea that love can grow gives children the opportunity to participate in devising ways and means to make it grow.

We get on well with all our grandchildren. We see them most weeks and I suppose we do spoil them. When our daughter adopted the twins – they were just four years old, the same as our youngest grandson – we got all our grandchildren together and worked out how to make the twins feel they belonged. The children had some good ideas and it made them include the twins straight away. My oldest grand-daughter was nearly 15 and she kind of took charge. I think the twins learned about grandparents from the other children. They soon expected special treats along with the rest of them but you could see that it really made them happy.
Grandparent with nine grandchildren, two adopted

This grandmother has photographs of all her grandchildren displayed in her sitting room. The adopted twins have been put right in the centre of the display.

What is meant by "behavioural problems"?

When children are said to have behavioural problems, it usually means more than high spirits, toddler temper tantrums, adolescent rudeness, routine naughtiness or just being stroppy. Children who feel rejected or insecure, who have been neglected or abused, who lack a sense of continuity or self-worth, will communicate their pain through their behaviour. In other words: if children are disturbed, their behaviour will become disturbing; if they feel they have no control over their own lives, they will attempt to impose control on others by any means in their power.

Lying, stealing, bed-wetting, soiling, unprovoked anger and aggression or complete withdrawal are symptoms of distress and cries for help. Very often a child's emotional development is arrested by bad experiences. Any of the behaviours listed above might be acceptable for a three-year-old, but would be considered as problematic for an older child.

When my brother and his wife adopted Cindy, they were over the moon. Then she started all this business with screaming if she didn't get her own way. She clings to my sister-in-law, won't leave her alone for a minute. She can't play on her own and she upsets other children. It's embarrassing because she behaves like a baby though she's a big girl. Last birthday I took them all out to the seaside with my children and we had a really good day. For once Cindy didn't try to get the others into trouble – they all got on like an ordinary family. Then on the way home, she got cross for no reason and did her screaming all the way back and upset everybody. She spoiled the outing. And you can never get her to say 'sorry'.
Uncle of adopted girl of nine

Children who have been hurt find it very hard to show remorse when they hurt others. If they feel bad about themselves, they may have to spoil anything good that happens to them because they feel they don't deserve it and they can't trust that it will last. It took Cindy three years in a loving home before she felt secure enough to act her age and to enjoy herself without spoiling the day at the end.

Many families experience an initial "honeymoon" when children are first placed for adoption. It can take some while for a child to feel safe enough to reveal their troubled self. There is hardly ever a straight course between problems and resolution of problems. There may be times of relative calm interspersed with difficulties; there may be consistent progress with three steps forward and two steps back; there may be a trouble-free run of years only to be followed by a particularly turbulent adolescence.

Grandparents and other relatives can show that they understand why a child behaves in a certain way while at the same time supporting the parents to hang on and to get through it. They can best support the children by accepting that they are stuck at a certain stage of emotional development and by having faith that they will not remain stuck there forever.

How will we cope with a disabled child?

If single parents or couples adopt a child with disabilities, they will have had the opportunity to think long and hard about the changes a disabled child will bring to the family. Ideally, the plan to adopt a child with disabilities will also have been discussed with grandparents and other relatives who may become involved. It is important to add a disabled child to the family not "in spite of" but "because of" the disability.

I explained to my family that we wanted to adopt Ricky because he was a baby with Down's Syndrome. We've been ordinary parents to ordinary children and we were ready to do something for a special child who needed a family more. My dad kept saying it was second best but it wasn't. It was best for Ricky and it was best for us. Now he's best for the whole family.
Adoptive parent

Another adoptive mother explained that just as every child is unique, so is every disability:

What you have to do is to find the beauty spot – that something or other that makes each child special. For me it's Joe's silence that says more than if he could speak.

Relatives by adoption may also be able to find the beauty spot of children with disabilities.

What about children from overseas?

Children adopted from overseas may be younger than most children needing adoption in the UK. However, they are even more likely to have suffered severe emotional and physical deprivation in early infancy. They may be from a different ethnic background than the adoptive family; they may speak or be used to hearing a different language; they may be familiar with a different religion, with different customs, food and climate. If children are adopted from overseas, they will grow up in their new family with three basic questions: Why didn't my parents keep me? Why didn't my people keep me? Why didn't my country keep me? This is a heavy load to carry into a new life. Grandparents and other relatives can help to support children from overseas by learning about their country and valuing their culture, so that they can grow up with pride in their origins and confidence in their status as adopted people and citizens of an adopted country.

What help is available?

Adoption law in England and Wales requires all adoption agencies to agree an adoption support plan when a child is placed with a new family. Adoption support can come in a variety of ways and from various directions. Specialist workers from social services, health and education can make valuable contributions. Both material and practical support should be available until the child is 18 – later if the young person is disabled.

Being prepared to accept help is as important as having the right help available. Sometimes adopters can feel that they have failed as parents if they ask for help. Or relatives can imply that there is something "wrong" if the adopted child is referred for therapy. Play therapy, drama therapy, art therapy and psychotherapy can guide a confused child towards putting their life together and help the parents and the extended family to support the child.

I was shocked when my son told me Ailsa was going to be seen at the clinic by a therapist. No one in the family has ever needed anything like that. She went twice a week for more than a year. My son and his wife used to go to see another person. I can see the improvement though I was against it.
Adoptive grandparent

Grandparents and other relatives can play a vital role in providing adoption support, not least by reassuring the parents that it is normal to seek outside help. After all, even grandparents can seldom draw on their own experience when adoption issues arise.

Will adopted stepchildren be my grandchildren/ nieces/nephews?

If the caretaking parent remarries, the new husband or wife can apply to adopt the children as long as the other birth parent agrees. Adopted stepchildren have the same legal status in the family as any other adopted children or, indeed, children born to the family.

In many cases there are more appropriate ways than adoption to secure the future for children from previous relationships. The Adoption and Children Act 2002 encourages stepfamilies to consider alternative arrangements to adoption in order to preserve the legal connection with the absent parent. Grandparents and other relatives then have to negotiate how best to include the children of previous marriages or partnerships in the extended family. Much will depend on the attitudes and expectations of the parents and on the existing extended families of the children.

How do relatives fit in if gay or lesbian couples or single parents adopt?

By the time Gail and I decided to adopt, my parents had long accepted her into the family. They greeted our announcement with the supportive trepidation with which they tended to greet all my "Big Plans". My parents had no grandchildren when we started on the adoption trail, so they were excited at the prospect but a little nervous

*about what kind of rollercoaster ride I intended to
take them on. My father thought it good that we
were going to be out because he is absolutely
obsessed with being honest. At the same time, he
was worried about how homophobic society is,
and concerned that we might face a lot of hurt
and disappointment. It was hard for them to see
the struggle we had at times during the process.*
From *Is it True you have Two Mums?* by Ruby Clay,
BAAF, 2010

Children grow up successfully in all kinds of families. Lesbian and
gay partners can adopt jointly throughout the UK, and there is
evidence that they can be excellent parents and that they and their
children need the support of relatives as much as other parents do.
It is, of course, important to know and to respect how the parents
tell their story and how the child understands it. Children will feel
comfortable in almost any truly caring situation as long as the adults
are comfortable and co-operative. Criticism or disapproval of the
parents' lifestyle, however covert, will not do; it would be better to
deal with any negative attitudes before attempting to build a
relationship with an adopted child.

*I couldn't see how they would let my son adopt. I
was worried about the boy turning out gay and
social services blaming my son. I was sort of
ashamed about being his grandmother and I made
him call me by my first name. This went on for a
long time, it must have been five years, till the boy
himself said to me: 'I haven't got a mother but I'd
like for you to be my grandmother'. I realised then
that I'd been his grandmother in all but name and
that he and my son were more clever about it than
I was.*
Grandparent of adopted teenager

What happens if an adoption doesn't work out?

Families and children have to know from the beginning of the adoption adventure that, in spite of the best of intentions and the best of preparation, there can be no guarantee that every adoption will work, because no one can really know how it will be and how it will feel when this child moves in with this family. If an adoption breaks down, it is good practice to call it a "disruption". This means that it is not the end of the road for a child but an interruption in the child's journey to a permanent placement.

A disruption is hardly ever anyone's fault. It is usually a combination of unidentified, misinterpreted, and unpredictable circumstances. For instance: no one knew the extent of abuse the child had suffered, the adopters were less tolerant of deviant behaviour than expected and the promised therapeutic support did not materialise. The most common causes of disruption are incomplete information, inaccurate assessments of trauma and loss and inadequate resources. We may have to stand by while seemingly promising placements crumble, but more often we can watch in respectful admiration as children and parents, with incalculable effort and patience, make the most improbable placements for adoption last.

If disruption becomes inevitable, it will be painful for all concerned, and that includes the relatives by adoption. Anger, guilt, resentment, shame and bewilderment are the feelings on the surface, and depression lurks beneath.

---

*My daughter and son-in-law adopted a little boy
aged five, a year ago. He was very difficult to
manage but I loved him like my own grandchild
and I think he loved me. He didn't ever settle down
and my daughter couldn't take it any more. He
used to hit her and spit at her and shout that she
wasn't his real mummy. He was better with my
son-in-law and in school and he was always better*

---

*with me but that only made it worse. She had all
the help there was and she tried everything they
said, but nothing worked. He was taken away by
social services. I know he's been placed with
another family but I don't know where. I can't
speak to my daughter about it because she just
clams up or bursts out crying. I feel I've lost my
only grandson and he's lost me. How could they
do it?*
Grandparent after disruption

When a placement is beyond help, adopters may have to give up
for the child's sake as well as their own. The only way to make
disruption less traumatic at the end is to manage it as carefully as
the introductions at the beginning. The child and family (including
the grandmother above) need an intensive period of preparation for
disruption, as well as support to maintain contact and continuity
after the child has moved. If the adopters have been badly wounded
and fear that they have damaged the child, they may want to cut
off completely. If grandparents and other relatives, who may
themselves be hurting, can show sympathy and understanding
for the parents, a cut-off may be avoided.

09

Katie's framily

We all think of ourselves as aunties and uncles and cousins – as a network. However, we aren't related by blood. We have separate friendships, but this network is our strongest and closest. We have known each other for many years and have experienced highs and lows together.

On a bright Sunday morning in autumn, 19 people gather in the living room of Louise and Rick, the proud adoptive parents of Katie, aged two. It isn't a very large living room, but there are enough comfortable chairs and sofas for everyone to get up close and, of course, the nine children in the group prefer sitting on the floor. These are the people who make up Katie's network, and it is not at all unusual for them to get together in this way, but on this occasion they have gathered to tell their story.

The story begins long before Katie was adopted. Both sets of grandparents belong to this group; the others are Louise's and Rick's lifelong friends and their children – three of them already grown up. Some of the adults have known each other since they were infants and all the children consider themselves like "cousins at least", as one of them said. Louise and Rick are godparents to some of them and special auntie and uncle to all of them, because until Katie arrived they were the only childless couple in the group with more time to spare for special activities and treats. But in fact all the women have always been "the aunties" for each other's children and now they are Katie's.

There is nothing formal or organised about this group: they all get together for special events, some families share holidays, the "aunties" regularly meet in pairs or trios or quartets: 'It feels like a sisterhood among the girls.' Some members live close to each other and see each other daily, they all support each other, listen to each other's stories and look out for each other's children. And the children are happy to spend time with their "aunties" without their own parents being there.

I feel everyone in my family accepts me for who I am and they don't judge me.
Alice, aged 12

All the members of the group know each other well enough to draw on each other's strengths and offer advice only when it is needed. *We have learned when to give advice and when not to, when to speak and when to hold our tongue.* They call themselves the "framily": a group made up of family and friends. They have created a virtual village in defiance of modern life.

It doesn't matter if it's early morning or late at night – we know we are there for each other. We can discuss any issue – we have really open and honest conversations, although what's said in the group stays in the group.

When Louise and Rick decided to adopt, the group was with them every step of the long, emotional journey that lasted four years from the time of the initial application to being matched with Katie.

Adoption

It's not fair, it takes nine months to make a baby and it's taking so long for Auntie Louise and Uncle Rick to have their child.
Oliver, aged 12

Louise and Rick shared the adoption process with the group. Everyone understood what was happening. Long before Katie was even born, the children did a "Build a Bear" workshop and made a bear for the new child-to-be, which they all signed.

Two of the women attended a Family and Friends training day offered regularly by the local authority working with Louise and Rick. They found it really helpful as it threw up issues they hadn't thought of, and they could share what they had learned with the wider group to ensure that the adopting couple had the best possible support around them. Both sets of parents, now Katie's grandparents, and two other members of the group were referees. After Louise and Rick were approved to adopt, everyone expected a child to be placed with them fairly quickly. After all, this was to be a third generation adoption: Louise was adopted and so was her father – no problem.

But third time round it took another two years. During that period there were several disappointments, with five links not progressing to a viable match. It was a stressful time. Louise said that it felt like having five miscarriages in a row. The waiting was hard on the network children. Each of them had been prepared to expect another child and they became impatient and couldn't understand why it was taking so long. It was hard for the adults too, especially for the grandparents-in-waiting, to see the couple go through so much pain and disappointment and to feel powerless to help them. There seemed to be no reason for such a long delay. They were all aware of the growing tensions and were careful not to dwell on the subject of adoption unless Louise and Rick raised it, and they tried to get on with doing fun things together.

We knew they were having doubts about whether to continue, but we didn't want a child to miss the opportunity to have these amazing parents and for them to have children, so we supported them to carry on even through the moments of doubt and the really hard times. Although it did take a long time, it meant that when Katie was eventually placed with Louise and Rick, it was like the best feeling ever!

Louise relied heavily on the group while she and Rick bore each disappointment and waited for a child, but at the same time they agreed not to discuss any more potential links with the network until there was a definite match. So when Katie was mentioned to them, they didn't speak about her until they had met with her social worker and her foster carer and knew that they were the only adopters being considered for Katie.

Katie arrives

When they knew Katie was finally coming to live with Auntie Louise and Uncle Rick, some of the children were concerned that their own relationship with them would change and that they might not see them as much, or be loved as much. They were assured that 'There is definitely enough love to go round'. And Katie quickly became the adored youngest member of the "framily".

Katie is the youngest in our "framily" now, but I was the youngest before Katie came. I was really excited as it meant I had someone to look after who was younger than me. Katie is my little special cousin and it's different to the friends I have at school. Katie's more close to me because we share lots of fun times together outside school and our mums are all really close.
Tom, aged 8

When Katie arrived, aged six months, everyone met her individually in her new home – grandparents first. She wasn't "passed around" or overwhelmed by the whole group; the "framily" respected that she had first to feel safe being held by her new parents, that she had to get used slowly to her new environment and that they shouldn't ask too many questions about Katie's past. They knew that Louise and Rick would share what they could, and what was appropriate, when they felt ready.

Everyone in the network is careful about what they say to other people and respect the fact that 'The people outside the network, who don't know the background, don't need to know'. They stress the difference between secrecy and privacy; when asked, the children say that Katie is their cousin. Ruby, aged 14, explains: 'It's her information, not ours, and one day Katie can decide whether to say she's adopted.'

On a day-to-day level we don't think about Katie as an adopted child – she is just "our Katie". But we did think about some of the important things about adoption, like not crowding her and allowing enough space for Louise and Rick to bond with Katie. Although she was very young, it was different to people bringing a new baby home. But they said it was strange for us not to be there, because they are used to having us all in their lives on such a regular basis. So we let them guide us as to when they wanted or needed to see us. They did need some practical and emotional support from us at this intense time.

How the network supports Katie and her parents

During the early days, while Louise and Rick were concentrating on Katie, one couple from the network brought food and cooked a hot meal while the parents were bathing the baby. Others helped with the washing, ironing and shopping. When asked, they gave advice on baby equipment and parenting strategies. Louise discovered that looking after an infant day and night is not the same as having children for sleepovers and being everyone's loving auntie.

Katie was a clingy baby, because in their determination to enable her to form a strong bond with them, the new parents hugged her and held her for a good deal of time, and picked her up whenever she cried. Whilst they were thrilled that Katie became quickly and firmly attached to them, they foresaw that it would be hard to leave her with anyone else in due course. Enter the "framily". They introduced some brief and well managed "separation" experiences, which began with Louise and Katie meeting some of the "aunties" and some of the "cousins" in the park. After a while, Louise would say 'Mummy be back soon'. To begin with she would just go off for half an hour, and then gradually she built it up to leaving her for a morning or an afternoon. Katie began to trust that Mummy always

came back when she said she would. By the end of Louise's
adoption leave, Katie was having a great time with her grandparents
and the aunties and cousins.

---

*We play with Katie a lot, and because we are so much older, but
still children, she seems to love to spend time with us. When she
came first, she was very clingy to Auntie Louise, but now she
knows us very well and she can't wait to have cuddles when she
sees us. And she doesn't get upset when Auntie Louise leaves
her at our house. She waves at her through the window and has
a wonderful time here – she is always really pleased to see
Auntie Louise when she picks her up though!*
Beth, aged 13

Now that Louise is working part-time again, Katie spends two days
a week with her maternal grandparents and her paternal
grandparents step in whenever they are needed; latterly they have
collected her from nursery when Louise has had to work extra
hours. At other times, if both Louise and Rick are working, one of
the "aunties" will take Katie out for the day, which she loves. It's a
kind of role reversal for them, because for so long Louise and Rick
were the "fun auntie and uncle".

One of the "framily" boys is an only child. He used to ask for a
brother or sister every birthday and Christmas until Katie came
along. Now he has stopped asking. He says: 'I know we say we're
cousins, but Katie is more like a little sister to me because she is the
closest I'll ever get to having a sister and she wears a special top hat
that says "little sister" when she comes to visit me.'

One of the older "framily" girls has decided she will adopt her
children when she grows up.

Celebration

A little while ago, there was a very special "framily" party. The stress of the adoption process was forgotten, the adoption order had been celebrated and now Katie was two years old. It was an afternoon tea party with old-fashioned children's games and a seaside theme – because the "framily" loved their outings to the seaside. Of course, everyone brought party food to share and Louise had a cake made to look like the seaside.

There was a "piñata" in the shape of a teapot and the children used up a lot of energy hitting it until the sweets cascaded out, to Katie's delight. Half of the children dressed up as waitresses and waiters and took orders from the adults and the other half, in chef's gear, made up the orders and created the drinks. Katie was experiencing life as it would go on.

There are many celebrations in the life of the "framily" – some are planned and some are spontaneous because one of the network has a idea. On the night before Christmas Eve, six of the "framily's" children will come and stay with Louise and Rick because they all want to see Katie's face when she comes downstairs in the morning to see the lighted Christmas tree in the decorated living room.

Some tips from adults in the network

- It's a big shock when social workers exit your life after having had such a huge involvement, so you will lean on your support network a lot in those early days.
- Don't be intimidated by adoption. Although you have to consider privacy and bonding and contact with the birth family, it is essentially a parenting task at the end of the day. I adopted Louise, and my daughter is my daughter, adopted or not.
- Please don't treat adopted children any differently – don't label

them. I was adopted and have lived my whole life not thinking too much about adoption, although it is always there in the background. Most of the time adoption doesn't come into your relationships with family and friends.

- If you are supporting people going through the adoption process, just have lots of patience and good listening skills.
- Be aware that adoption is a long process, and during that process, adoptive parents have to dig deep emotionally and things can come to the surface that are unexpected, and you have to understand that they might or might not want to talk about it.
- Be careful about the pressure you can put on prospective adopters by asking intrusive questions. You have to give them the space and time to share things at their own pace. A lot of the time they just want to get on with life.
- Offer emotional support. Be there at the end of the phone. Recognise that they may go from not having had children to suddenly being parents of a child, not necessarily a baby, so be prepared to offer practical support as well.
- Think positively about adoption; when I was little, I wished I had been adopted because I was told Louise was special because she was adopted.
- Learn as much as you can about the process and adoption in general.
- Adopters will come to different people in the network for different things at different times.

What the children say

- Adoption is one of the best things that can happen in your life.
- When you ask a lot of questions you can make it worse for them.
- Adoption means not treating them any different – just with a lot of love and care.
- Be very kind to the child because they have had a difficult time.

- Auntie Louise did a slide show of Katie's first year with them. And my grandma said that in every photo everyone looked so happy with a beaming smile on their faces, which sums up the joy Katie has brought to our "framily" (Will, aged 13).

The last word should go to Louise:

The genetic link is not the most important thing. We are not connected by blood to our partners with whom we have the closest relationships. It's about Katie's life and her relationships and that will always include her very special "framily".

10

Endpiece:
What you can do

She was our first grandchild. We didn't know anything about adoption, we didn't know what was expected of us or what we could manage. It was like taking a leap into the unknown – but it was worth it.
Parents of adopters

What do you want to do? What do you think you should do? What can you do?

Not every grandparent, aunt, uncle or cousin will want to be involved if someone in the family plans to adopt. All relations, including grandparents, will have their own life to lead and the family style may be to remain related at a distance, whether children are born into the family or adopted. Before making a commitment to support the prospective adopters, it is wise to ask yourself: 'What do I want to do?' Do you want to be actively involved wherever possible? Or do you want to be included only if needed and say what you think only if asked? Do you want to offer regular help with child care or just occasional babysitting? Do you want to be indispensable or merely available?

Don't let yourself be too much influenced by what you think you should do. Having children by adoption, like having children by birth, has to be the responsibility of the parents. It may be lovely if the family is the kind of family that rallies round, but not all families do, and some parents may prefer it if they don't. There is no reason why you should respond to an adoption in the family in any other way than to a birth. If you find it difficult to respond in the same way, because the child is not related to you, then give yourself time. It's no help trying to tell yourself how you ought to feel, if you don't. It's a good enough start to treat an adopted child with the respect, kindness and consideration you would normally show to anyone who came to stay with your family.

What you want to do and what you think you should do may not be quite the same as what you can do. You may be asking too much of yourself; there may be family conflicts, which get in the way; distances between family members may be too daunting; or you may simply have to earn a living. It is important not to raise expectations of help and support too high, before a child arrives, if there is a danger of having to let adopters and children down later.

I wish now that I'd not promised to look after him in the mornings while my daughter works. I hadn't looked after a little one for so long and he was all over the place and it wore me out. I had to tell her – it caused a lot of bad feeling. She's still upset with me and Social Services blame her for not sorting it out beforehand and I blame myself because the little one's been put in a nursery now and he doesn't like it.
Mother of single adopter

Better to restrict yourself, from the beginning, to what you know you can manage. It is easier then for adopters to make arrangements for the support they will need. And reading to a child, each time you visit, can be as rewarding for both of you as daily childcare. One eight-year-old wrote in class: *'When grandparents read to us they don't skip and they don't mind if we ask for the same story again'*.

Stories have made many appearances in this brief book. There are the stories children bring into new families and the stories families have to tell. These are the stories that get woven together into the adoption story. And the adoption story grows and, like all good stories, gets handed down from one generation to the next. Stories bear witness to the continuity of people and of communities. Everyone has their very own story and adds layers to the stories of others. Relatives by adoption have a contribution to make to the adoption story and their own stories will become enriched by the adoption experience. Adopted children, like all children, love to have relations. As another eight-year-old in the same class wrote:

Everybody should try to have a grandmother or grandfather or aunt or uncle, especially if they don't have television, because they are the only grown-ups who have spare time to spend with us.

Useful organisations

ADOPTION UK
A UK-wide self-help group supporting adoptive families before, during and after adoption.
Linden House
55 The Green
South Bar Street
Banbury
Oxfordshire OX16 9AB
Tel: 01295 752240
www.adoptionuk.org.uk

BRITISH ASSOCIATION FOR ADOPTION AND FOSTERING (BAAF)
A UK-wide organisation for everyone who works in adoption, fostering and childcare.
Saffron House
6–10 Kirby Street
London EC1N 8TS
Tel: 020 7421 2600
www.baaf.org.uk

FAMILY RIGHTS GROUP (FRG)

A national organisation that advises on family law and childcare practice.
The Print House
18 Ashwin Street
London E8 3DL
Advice line: 0808 801 0366
www.frg.org.uk

GRANDPARENTS' ASSOCIATION

A self-help group supporting grandparents.
Moot House
The Stow
Harlow
Essex CM20 3AG
Helpline: 0845 434 9585
www.grandparents-association.org.uk

GRANDPARENTS PLUS

A national organisation that offers consultation and training for grandparents, plus other relatives and professionals.
18 Victoria Park Square
Bethnal Green
London E2 9PF
Tel: 020 8981 8001
www.grandparentsplus.org.uk